THE RAIL
ACCIDENT AT
NORTON FITZWARREN, 1940

by A.R. Kingdom

ARK PUBLICATIONS
(RAILWAYS)

First published in 2005 by ARK PUBLICATIONS (RAILWAYS), an imprint of
FOREST PUBLISHING, Woodstock, Liverton, Newton Abbot, Devon TQ12 6JJ

Copyright © A. R. Kingdom 2005

British Library Cataloguing in Publication Data
A catalogue record for this book is available from the British Library
ISBN 1–873029–10–1

23 KILLED IN WEST EXPRESS DISASTER

56 INJURED IN HOSPITAL

Service Men, Women, And Children Among The Casualties

CRASH NOT DUE TO ENEMY ACTION OR SABOTAGE

MORE than sixteen hours after an express from Paddington to Penzance met with disaster at Norton Fitzwarren, near Taunton, early yesterday, police, soldiers, and A.R.P. workers were still digging among the wreckage to find three bodies believed to be under the debris.

The official list of the dead issued last night showed a total of 23. They include eight sailors and two women. It is believed that the bodies of two children of one of the women victims and the body of the fireman are among those yet to be recovered.

The death-roll is the biggest in a rail crash for three years.

There are 56 injured—some in a serious condition—in the Taunton and Somerset Hospital.

The derailment of the engine and three coaches, through some at present unknown cause, was a "pure accident," and not the result of enemy action or sabotage.

Single-line working was in operation past the scene of the accident last night.

Reproduced courtesy of the *Western Morning News*

ARK PUBLICATIONS (RAILWAYS)
Editorial, layout and design by:
Mike Lang

Typeset by:
Carnaby Typesetting, Torquay, Devon TQ1 1EG

Printed and bound in Great Britain by:
The Printing Press, 21 Clare Place, Coxside, Plymouth PL4 0JW

Cover photographs:

Front – A view looking towards Taunton of No. 6028 *King George VI* and the severely damaged coaches at the front end of the train. Recovery has already commenced.

Western Morning News

Back – The track layout at the western end of Norton Fitzwarren Station looking towards Plymouth in September 1945. To the left of the picture is the fateful 'down' relief line, which at the time of the accident terminated at a point opposite the start of the Barnstaple branch seen going off to the right.

Peter W. Gray

CONTENTS

ACKNOWLEDGEMENTS

The author is indebted to the following in the production of this book.

Mrs R. W. Christison for placing at his disposal the detailed notes and records of her late husband, Mr A. W. H. Christison, District Motive Power Superintendent, British Rail (Western Region).

British Railways Board for permission to reproduce the official photographs and accident inquest data of the Chief Engineer's and Drawing Offices of the former Great Western Railway Co.

The Somerset County Gazette; The Somerset County Herald; The Western Morning News.

The Reference Libraries at Plymouth and Taunton.

Bryan Gibson; Peter Gray; Mike Lang; Mike Willis.

DEDICATION

This book is dedicated to all railwaymen and women who kept our trains running throughout the Second World War. Their task was immense, carried out often in the Stygian gloom of the wartime 'blackout'. The railways were sometimes bombed and straffed by enemy fighters. Staff worked very long hours, often with little sleep or any kind of respite. In many cases their homes were damaged or destroyed by enemy bombing (as was the home of the driver of our train), and yet they carried on regardless, keeping vital supplies and servicemen and women constantly on the move.

In my opinion, however, at the end of the war they were all quickly forgotten and received little recognition for their contribution to our victory. They were, as far as I know, never represented at any victory or remembrance parades. In addition, sadly, their efforts were overshadowed by a post-war pay dispute and the subsequent nationalisation of the four main companies into British Railways on 1st January 1948.

As a very young man, I often travelled with my family during the war and I remember what it was like as a passenger! I hope this book will therefore serve to redress the balance and correct any lack of recognition of their efforts.

Finally, I dedicate it to all who lost their lives, or were injured, in the accident that occurred on that bleak day in November 1940.

A.R. Kingdom

INTRODUCTION

I first considered the contents of this book as part of a larger work in the 'Transport Topics' series for the Oxford Publishing Co. during the early 1980s. It was to recount no less than three accidents which befell the GWR and BR on the same stretch of line around Norton Fitzwarren – west of Taunton in Somerset – during the previous ninety years.

The first was on 11th November 1890, when the second of two special mail trains from Plymouth Millbay, serving the recently docked *Northam Castle*, crashed into a stationary (slow) 'down' goods train standing on the 'up main' line in Norton Station. It was parked there by the signalman to allow an express goods train heading for Plymouth to pass on the 'down main' line. In this accident eleven were killed and eight injured.

The second accident was on 4th November 1940 and is the subject of this book, while the third was in the early hours of 6th July 1978, when the overnight sleeper from Penzance to Paddington burst into flames as it approached Taunton Station. Again eleven died and some twenty were injured.

I abandoned the idea of covering all three accidents mainly because of the severe imbalance of information which was at my disposal. In 1890 cameras were a rare commodity and only two official photographs existed; these have already been much used in railway literature. Most of the copious reporting was in the minutely-detailed columns of the local press. The 1940 accident, on the other hand, was not only photographed and reported by the national and local press, but I was fortunate enough to have in my possession the official GWR inquest report, complete with detailed photographs. The 1978 accident, too, was well covered by both the local and the national press, added to which there was the 'sitting room' coverage of the television channels. However, as the accident was comparatively recent and a very sensitive issue, it was not considered prudent to include it in any book.

Ultimately I decided to present the 1940 accident in its entirety, but in such a manner as to dramatise the narrative, as opposed to simply writing it as a report, and to include certain assumptions based on my own wartime travelling experiences. I have also assumed in the absence of any documentary evidence to the contrary, and however unlikely it might seem with enemy aircraft in the night-time skies, that the train kept to its timetable until reaching the Bristol area.

Finally, I would stress that this book is not an attempt to capitalise upon the misfortunes of others, or to recall memories still painful to descendants of the train's crew, the GWR Company's operational staff of the time, and descendants of the victims' families. It is, however, a respectful attempt to illustrate the intensely detailed examination given to all accidents by the former railway companies, even during wartime (and at a particular time when our fortunes were at their lowest ebb) – a tradition carried on during nationalisation by the British Railways Board and now by the privatised railway companies in a never-ending search to make our railways the safest in the world.

A.R. Kingdom
March 2005

THE RAILWAY ACCIDENT AT NORTON FITZWARREN, 1940

Diary of Events

Preamble

By November 1940 we were fourteen months into the Second World War and things were going very badly for Britain. France had fallen earlier in the year without putting up any sort of a fight and left us to face the might of Hitler's armies alone. Thanks to the immense bravery of 'The Few' Britain had won a temporary reprieve from invasion following the final day of 'The Battle of Britain' on 15th September. On the home front, the government had taken control of the railway companies, whose system would play a major part in the war effort as the main arteries carrying the lifeblood of the nation – food, raw materials, munitions, troops and civilian passengers; indeed, cargoes of every kind. Trains were straffed and bombed and ran into all kinds of danger. Throughout all this our railwaymen and women worked tirelessly, often without adequate sleep or nourishment. Sadly, when the war was over, they received scant recognition for their efforts and the railways' infrastructure was left in a very worn-out state.

Sunday 3rd November 1940

"What a foul night for taking a train to Plymouth!", exclaimed Driver Stacey to Fireman Seabridge as they signed on for duty at Old Oak Motive Power Depot. "None worse", replied Fireman Seabridge. "Going back on duty again, it seems these days we are hardly off duty." "Yes, I have never worked so hard these last months", agreed Driver Stacey, "as soon as you arrive with one train, there's an all too short a break and another's waiting to be taken out. I hardly ever have any time with my family now, it's all work." The time was 8.25 p.m. on a very wet and windy night in wartime London's blackout on Sunday 3rd November 1940.

Once Driver Stacey and Fireman Seabridge had signed on for duty they were allocated their engine by the Shed Foreman. This time it was No. 6028 *King George VI*, already coaled, watered and fired by the depot staff. It stood simmering on one of the roads near the main shed.

A few moments later they climbed onto the footplate and commenced their respective tasks commensurate with the taking over of a steam locomotive. Fireman Seabridge opened the fire doors, which emitted a reddish glow on the underside of the blackout screen slung between the cab roof and the tender. He then raked over, checked and fed the fire, as well as checking the water level in the boiler, whilst Driver Stacey ensured that there was sufficient vacuum for the brakes before descending from the footplate onto the heavily-crusted tracks. Guided with the light from a flare lamp, his next task was to oil the motion and check to his satisfaction that everything was in mechanically good order.

By 9.25 p.m. they had both completed their tasks and were ready to move the engine, which by now had a full head of steam. Driver Stacey opened the cylinder cocks to allow any water that had condensed in the cylinders to be expelled and then, gently opening the regulator, slowly moved the locomotive out of the depot to pick up the running lines into Paddington. Fifteen minutes later they had backed No. 6028 onto a thirteen-coach train weighing in excess of 400 tons and coupled up, so forming the 9.50 p.m. express passenger train to Penzance via Bristol, which they had booked on to work as far as Plymouth.

Dead on time the signals came off and Passenger Guard Winyard who, like Driver Stacey, came from Acton, blew his whistle and showed 'a dim green' from his masked hand-lamp. This done, he boarded the eighth coach, closed the door and entered his guards compartment to prepare for the journey. Meanwhile, on the footplate, Fireman Seabridge busied himself with the fire, while Driver Stacey concentrated on the road ahead as the heavy train pulled out of the station: soon the environs of inner-London were being left behind, at an ever-quickening rate in the dense blackness of the night.

In quick succession came the well-known Ranelegh Bridge, Royal Oak and Westbourne Park; and then it was on past Old Oak Common Motive Power Depot, from whence they had set out. Still gathering speed, they stormed through Southall and Hayes, and pressed on towards Taplow, the exhaust echoing in the night air as it sped back over the train and then drifted away into the blackness. All the while the constantly-waving beams of the searchlights from twitchy defence batteries looking for any aircraft that might have been overhead lit the distant sky. Nevertheless, with the engine working hard, Maidenhead and Twyford were quickly passed and, by 10.35 p.m., the regulator was being closed and the brakes applied as the first stop, Reading, was reached, Here the main lines to Plymouth direct via Westbury and to Plymouth via Bristol diverged: the '9.50 p.m.' was taking the latter route and the 'right away' from Reading was given to it at 10.42 p.m.

Didcot was reached by 11.10 p.m. and the train was on its way again by 11.25 p.m., this stop allowing it to connect with the 11.15 p.m. local train to Oxford.

Monday 4th November 1940

Swindon (home of the GWR) was reached by 12.05 a.m., the train departing again after a stop of ten minutes. The quickest of stops followed at Chippenham – between 12.35 and 12.38 a.m. – and from there the train headed for Bath, its next stop. On arrival at Bath at 12.55 a.m., an eerie glow lit the sky over distant Bristol; it was an ominous warning of what was to come. Nevertheless, still on time at exactly 1.00 a.m., the train commenced the next leg of the journey to Bristol.

The timetable allowed only 15 minutes to reach Bristol, but there was now trouble brewing in the shape of an air raid. As a consequence of this, records do not show if the train was held up east of the city (the most likely scenario given the circumstances), in Temple Meads Station after its due arrival of 1.15 a.m., or, later, to the south of the city after the scheduled departing time of 1.25 a.m. The fact remains, beyond doubt, that Stacey and Seabridge's train was held up for an hour and eight minutes in the Bristol area and did not depart until 2.33 a.m. Fate was to decree that this delay sowed the seeds of a pending disaster.

The air raid must have had a devastating effect on Driver Stacey, as his house in Acton had been bombed only a few days earlier, making him and his family homeless. True to the unbreakable spirit of those dark days, he carried on with his vital work not knowing how his family were coping in his absence or, indeed, if they were suffering from further attacks on London.

At this juncture the author, with the kind permission of a fellow author and former GWR signalman, Adrian Vaughan, takes up the story with lines from his book *Grime & Glory – Tales of the GWR 1892 – 1947:–*

… the train was delayed and arrived in Taunton, on the down relief line, sixty-eight minutes late at 3.30 a.m.
All signals for main and relief lines westwards were at 'Danger' when Stacey ran in on 6028 because Signalman Wadham in West Station box could see a 'situation' developing. The 9.50 p.m. Paddington was scheduled to go away from relief to main line but the 12.50 a.m. Paddington to Penzance newspaper train [hauled by No. 6013 *King Henry VIII*], non-stop through Taunton on the down main, had been 'wired' as 'five early Westbury' and was now 'getting handy'. Wadham waited, leaning on his levers, watching the clock, waiting to see if the 9.50 Paddington would finish its station work in time to be allowed out, as booked, main line. At 3.36 a.m. he phoned Athelney box, 8 miles away. 'Got the Papers about, Bob?'
'Be by me in one,' came the surprising reply. The 12.50 was still picking up time. 'Let him run', thought Wadham to himself and asked [for] the road for the 9.50 down the relief line. He had just finished pulling the appropriate levers over when the signalman at Taunton East Junction [box] asked [for] the road down the main for the 12.50 Paddington. Wadham had first to get the road from West Junction [box] before he could give the road to East Junction [box] but then, from Cogload Junction [box] 4³/₄ miles to the east to Norton Fitzwarren 2 miles to the west, red lights changed to green and amber distant signal lights below them also went to green – except that on the relief line at Norton Fitzwarren the signals remained at 'Danger'.
Stacey got the 'right away' [from Taunton] at 3.43. He could not see the junction signal to his left at the platform end because of the length of the boiler but he could see the other signals away down

the track, double green lights on main and relief lines, and because he was scheduled to go out main line into his head came the fixation that he was signalled out onto the down main line. He whistled-up on 6028 and set sail along the down relief line. The 12.50 a.m. Paddington was flying down the main [line] between Cogload [Junction] and Creech [St Michael].

Stacey, inexplicably, was unaware of his situation. The line ahead was virtually straight and the well-spaced green lights of the relief and main lines shone brightly in the dark until the length of the boiler obscured the relief line signal at close range. Norton Fitzwarren's distant signal was at 'Caution' and gave him a siren [which would have sounded in the cab] 1677 yds before the throw-off points at the end of the relief line. He cancelled the siren and continued to accelerate. Signalman Tucker in Silkmill signal box was treated to the sight of the 'King'-hauled passenger train thundering down the slow line and the Papers, also 'King'-hauled with a mere five vans on, coming up on the 9.50's tail on the main line. It never occurred to him that the 9.50 was speeding somewhat considering that the end of its track was only 1000 yds away.

Bill Coles at Norton [Fitzwarren box] lowered his down relief line home signal when the 'approach track circuit' indicator swung round to 'Occupied'. To his utter amazement the 9.50 went tearing past as if it had the road to Plymouth as the 12.50 went by on the main line.

A disaster was unavoidable and about to happen! That in itself was bad enough, but that it should involve the locomotive named after the reigning king made it even more poignant given the parlous state of the nation at the time.

The Crash

At precisely 3.48 a.m. No. 6028 *King George VI*, weighing 89 tons, jumped over a ditch and fell onto the fireman's side of the locomotive in a field beyond the 'throw off' points. A rivet-head from its bogie-frame then shot, bullet-like, through the side of the fourth van of the newspaper train, while the rear guards van, as it cleared the scene of the accident, was showered with flying ballast. In the meantime, the leading coaches of the 9.50 p.m. telescoped against the tender and the others scattered, fan-wise, across the tracks as the 12.50 a.m.'s tail lamp disappeared around the bend. Guard Baggot of the 12.50 a.m. was alarmed by the hammering of the stones against his van and applied the brake, but neither he nor Driver Hawkings and Fireman Lindsey had any idea of their narrow escape until they were told by the signalman at Victory Siding signal box, where they were stopped.

One can barely imagine the scene on the footplate at the moment the locomotive, thrown off by the 'catch points', and leaving the rails, crashed onto its side into a field. Several hundredweight of coal was to cascade from its tender onto the footplate, trapping Fireman Seabridge under it, and what with this and escaping steam ejecting from strained joints on the cab fittings and hot coals from the firebox adding to the chaos it must have resembled a 'scene from hell'. Driver Stacey, himself flung with some force onto the piles of debris, must have thought his end had come.

After any human tragedy, there is always a brief instance of deadly silence before the cries of the trapped and injured ensue. True to his long experience and training as a footplate man, Driver Stacey extricated himself from the wreckage and jumped into the icy waters of the adjacent flooded field. Wading along the train in total blackness, his first thought was to 'protect his train'. This may seem to the uninitiated a belated and ironic act, but it meant in this case that he had to provide warning to other oncoming trains that the lines were blocked with wreckage. He, together with the train's guard, Winyard, also had to alert the nearest signalmen, detonators had to be placed on the line far enough away to give ample warnings, and the guard had to ensure red aspect lights were showing at both ends of the train.

The Aftermath – Newspaper Reports

(a) The Crash

REMARKABLE COINCIDENCES: 1890 DISASTER RECALLED

The number of persons killed in the G.W.R. express train disaster at Norton Fitzwarren in the early hours of Monday morning is so far known to be 27 and the number of injured, some of them seriously, 58.

This was the worst train accident in Britain for three years, and, by a strange coincidence, it occurred within about 200 yards of the last big railway disaster in West Somerset, which, also curiously enough, happened in the early hours of a November morning exactly fifty years ago – in 1890. On that occasion ten persons were killed and several injured.

Monday's accident, as most people will now know, was to a packed express passenger train which left Paddington for Penzance at 9.50 p.m. on Sunday, and which, running late, reached the scene of the accident, about 200 yards west of Norton Fitzwarren station, just before 4 a.m. It was pitch dark at the time, and there was blinding rain, grim accompaniments to the terrible scenes that were to follow so soon.

The heavy locomotive and five of the coaches, for some reason yet officially unexplained (this is a matter for the Ministry of Transport inquiry – which opened at Taunton yesterday), left the rails. The engine plunged on to its left side, and the first three coaches were telescoped. In these coaches were many naval men returning from leave in various parts of the country, and some civilians, and it was among these people that most of the casualties of dead and injured occurred.

The Railway Company hastened in an official statement to assure the public that there was no question of the accident having been caused by enemy action or sabotage; nor was it contributed to by a newspaper train which happened to be passing at the time.

RENDING CRASH

Only those who have visited the scene of a train smash can visualise what happened. At one moment a splendid train was gliding swiftly through the darkness. Then, suddenly, there was a rending crash, a terrifying upheaving of the engine and the front coaches; they plunged off the track and either turned over on their sides, as the engine did, or swerved athwart the track and crumpled, with wreckage scattering in many directions.

The cries of entrapped passengers and the hiss of steam added to the confusion, and there was death and agony in almost every part. What happened in the train itself is described by passengers in statements given below.

The first thought of the driver, a London man, who had been flung clear of his engine, was to stop all oncoming trains, so he stumbled up the line and had the signals placed at danger. His fireman, Mr. W. Seabridge, also of London, was under the engine and lost his life.

HELPERS APPEAR

Awakened by the noise of the crash, people in Norton village and around rushed to the scene. The Village Hall was opened up to receive casualties, and Mr. and Mrs. Fred Bailey at the Railway Inn handed over all their household linen for bandages.

Messages were sent to Taunton, and doctors from there and other places, the Taunton Men's V.A.D., ambulances, railwaymen, troops, and A.R.P. workers came in increasing numbers and set to work among the wreckage. The ambulances were drawn up at Norton Fitzwarren station.

As by the meagre light of torches, all that could be used, heavy crowbars and other tools were plied to the wreckage, ambulance men pulled out the dead, the dying, and the injured, while doctors, including two naval surgeons who were on the train as passengers, performed wonders on those alive. One man had a leg amputated while he was under the wreckage. The courage and fortitude of the injured and entrapped was impressive.

MOVING THE INJURED

The railwaymen worked hard on the battered coaches, and as casualties were taken out they were taken on stretchers to the ambulances, the seriously injured to be conveyed to Taunton Hospital and the dead to the Taunton Mortuary. Less serious cases were treated at the Norton Village Hall. And so the work of rescue and relief went on through the hours of darkness and throughout Monday.

SCENE DESCRIBED

A "Somerset County Herald" reporter was on the scene in the morning, and here is a word picture he gives of the scene: The engine lay on its left side, with the three telescoped coaches piled up behind; a mass of twisted iron and steel ploughed into the ground, blocking the rails to the boundary. Splintered woodwork was scattered over a big area of the track. Compartments were smashed to matchwood, and some of the wheels were completely wrenched off.

Scores of rescuers worked feverishly, among them the Chief Constable of Somerset, Mr. J. E. Ryall, and many soldiers, who formed a human chain to get luggage clear of the wreckage. Heavy rain had made many pools, but, heedless of everything, the doctors and others toiled on. The colloquialism of a constable standing by summed them up: "You have to hand it to these rescuers." At intervals a body would be taken out, or injured still alive, and Taunton ambulance men and women helpers carried them on stretchers steadily along the track to the waiting ambulances.

Trains passed slowly to and fro on a single-line system of working, and still the breakdown gangs continued levering and pulling until most of the dead and injured had been removed. Some of the train still remains, and it must be many days before the line can be cleared.

TWO CRANES USED

Two big cranes, which were eventually brought up from Swindon and Newton Abbot to assist in the salvage work, were used to remove bogeys, heavy pieces of steel, and other wreckage which hampered the efforts of the ambulance men.

The violence of the impact was evidenced by the manner in which the bogeys and steelworks were twisted. A solid block of stone, weighing several tons, lay by one of the coaches where bodies were found. It had formed part of a culvert and had been hurled forward about 30 feet.

PASSENGERS' STORIES

MANY THOUGHT IT WAS BOMBS

When the crash came many passengers were dozing. One said it seemed as though the front of his coach leapt up in the air. The back part of the train did not leave the rails, and most of the passengers in those coaches were unhurt.

THOUGHT IT WAS BOMBS

Many survivors told the same story, that the accident happened with such startling suddenness that they thought the express had been bombed, and because of this some instinctively dropped to the floor. Their action undoubtedly saved them from more serious injuries.

What happened after the crash was described by one of the injured passengers as a nightmare. People – Service men, women, and children – were trapped in the wreckage. Passengers who could do so scrambled out in the inky darkness.

There were many incidents of heroism among the injured. A sailor said: "I heard one poor fellow whose leg was doubled up and whose arm was missing say, 'I'm all right, mate. Give me a fag.' "

TRAPPED FOR SEVEN HOURS

A petty officer in the Navy was trapped for seven hours. He bore his ordeal with great fortitude, and spectators cheered when he was removed on a stretcher.

"The doctors and the A.R.P. workers, especially the women, were magnificent," said one spectator. "They had a gruelling job, but they stuck to it."

The Railway Inn and the Village Hall at Norton Fitzwarren were used as casualty clearing centres. Women in the village worked throughout the early hours of the morning making tea for the rescuers and injured.

"A NIGHTMARE"

A sailor who was travelling in the third coach from the engine said he was dozing when the crash occurred.

"What followed was a nightmare," he said. "In the compartment next to mine five people were injured and two were killed. Everyone worked like Trojans to free those who had been trapped. I got a woman out, and I saw another sailor, his face covered with blood, struggle clear clasping a baby. The injured people showed great pluck."

A railwayman described how an 11-years-old boy, after being carried from a wrecked coach, insisted on going back to get the family luggage.

Several sleeping children were brought out uninjured.

After working throughout the morning, breakdown gangs had recovered 20 bodies from the wreckage, and they were taken to Taunton A.R.P. mortuary.

HOW TAUNTON MEN ESCAPED

Two Taunton Naval men, who were returning in the express from week-end leave, had remarkable escapes. They were Petty Officer R. W. Pring, of 36, Albermarle-road, and Acting Petty Officer Alfred George Waddon, of 28, Laburnum-street. They were together in the first compartment next to the engine.

Mr. Waddon, who has been twice torpedoed during the war, broke his leg in the rail accident, and Mr. Pring received a compound fracture of the right ankle.

They are believed to be the only survivors out of 16 men who were in the first two or three compartments.

Mr. Waddon probably owes his life to the fact that Mr. Pring had a torch which he repeatedly flashed against the window of the telescoped compartment until it attracted rescuers.

Up to that time Mr. Waddon appears to have been in danger of being suffocated. A mass of wreckage and at least one body had to be removed before he could be got out.

Mr. Pring was trapped for nearly five hours.

WIFE STAYED AT HOME.

His wife, who has recently been staying with him at Plymouth, told a representative of this paper she had intended going back on the express, but her husband advised her to "hang on and travel in daylight."

Mrs. Pring added that if their son at Taunton had not been feeling unwell at the time she would have been with her husband on the train.

HOSPITAL STAFF "WORKED WONDERS."

The praise of a Bristol sailor for the work of doctors and nurses at the hospital knew no bounds, nor could he speak too highly of the many kindnesses he himself received during his stay there.

"The staff worked wonders here yesterday in dealing with the rush of casualties," he told a representative of this paper on Tuesday. "All the injured seem bright and cheerful to-day, and it is surprising what a change I can see in them already."

Mrs. Pring, wife of Petty Officer Pring, echoed his sentiments when she stated, "The doctors and nurses at the hospital were really marvellous."

Some of them were on duty for 24 hours without rest.

Taunton V.A.D. nurses, who were called upon to augment the regular staff at the hospital to cope with the pressure of work, stood the test very well indeed, and certainly proved their worth in an emergency.

WOMEN DRIVE AMBULANCES.

Some of the ambulances in use for many hours after the fatality were driven by women, and members of the Women's Voluntary Service rendered valuable help in various ways.

Blood transfusions for some of the most serious cases were given at the hospital on Monday by members of the Taunton Blood Transfusion Service.

PATHETIC REUNIONS

Telegrams were sent on Monday to relatives of injured persons believed to be on the danger list, together with a notification that if necessary their fares to Taunton would be paid. Relatives and friends began to arrive the same evening, and there were pathetic reunions.

Others had the painful ordeal of identifying bodies in the A.R.P. mortuary at Union Gate, opposite the hospital.

WAS IN PLATE BATTLE.

Miss Gladys Hemmens, of Bristol, visited her fiance, First-class Stoker Arthur Martin, of 13, Vale-lane, Bristol, 3, who had injuries to the face, arm, and foot. He is believed to have lost several toes.

She said that he was with H.M.S. Exeter in the River Plate battle, and received a shrapnel wound in his shoulder.

"Yesterday," she said, "we received a wire saying he was dangerously ill. He lives at home with his mother, who is totally blind, and when I get back I shall be able to tell her that Arthur is in wonderful spirits. I know that will comfort her."

Miss Hemmens was at the hospital at the same time as Mrs. Pring, who kindly accommodated her for the night.

Extracted (as written) from the *Somerset County Herald*
Saturday, November 9, 1940

(b) The Inquest

"ERROR OF JUDGMENT" VERDICT

A Taunton jury of nine men, at the close of an inquest lasting nearly seven hours on Tuesday, unanimously agreed that there was an "error of judgment, certainly not criminal" by the driver of the Paddington – Penzance night express, which crashed at Norton Fitzwarren at about 3.50 a.m. on November 4th.

It was revealed that the driver was looking at the wrong signals, being unaware that his train had been diverted to the relief line to allow the newspaper train to pass on the main line.

The inquest concerned the deaths of 27 passengers on the train, which was carrying about 900 persons. A total of 68 were injured, 58 of them being detained in hospital.

JURY'S VERDICT

NOT A CRIMINAL ERROR.
The Foreman, Mr. G. W. Small, announced the jury's verdict as follows:–
"We find that the engine driver has been guilty of an error of judgment, but we cannot decide on the actual degree of error. It was certainly not criminal, especially in view of the abnormal weather and other conditions."
The driver, Mr. Percy William Stacey, of 54, Noel-road, Acton, stated, in his evidence, that until he saw the newspaper train passing on the main line at Norton Fitzwarren, he did not realise he was on the relief line.
Other evidence was given that the express usually travelled on the main line.
The jury added this rider to their verdict: "It appears to us that some arrangement of communication should be made to the driver of any train entering this relief line contrary to the usual procedure."
DIFFICULT JOURNEY.
The Coroner, in his address to the jury, before they retired, said: "The engine driver had a difficult journey all the way from London owing to the bad weather, the mist and black-out, I think he definitely made an error.
"Do you think there is some excuse for the error, or do you think he has been grossly negligent? If you have any doubt in your minds you should obviously resolve it in his favour."
EIGHT FOOT MODEL.
An eight-foot long model of the rail track at Norton Fitzwarren, complete with coloured signals and signal boxes, was displayed for the guidance of the jury, who had officially visited the scene of the crash.
Mr. P. W. Pine represented the Great Western Railway Company.
Mr. J. G. Baty, organising secretary A.S.L.E. & F., Bristol, represented Driver Stacey, the relatives of his fireman, Mr. W. Seabridge, London (who was killed at his post) and the relatives of Mr. C. H. James, G. W. R.

engine driver, Acton, who was a passenger on the train and was killed.

Mr. H. Collins, western district organiser of the National Union of Railwaymen, Bristol, represented local signalmen.

Mr. F. S. Dodson and Mr. Frank Birch (Taunton) and Mr. J. McGahey (Exeter) appeared for relatives of several victims.

Police Supt. Edwards was also present.

COMPANY ADMIT LIABILITY.

The Coroner pointed out, in opening the inquiry, that the Great Western Railway Company had admitted liability so far as any claims were concerned. Solicitors representing relatives of victims, therefore, would not ask the number of questions that they would otherwise have felt it their duty to ask.

Women relatives of several of the dead wept silently as Dr. Godfrey Carter, pathologist, gave evidence of the terrible injuries. Nearly all the victims, he said, died from multiple injuries. Death in many cases, in his opinion, was instantaneous and several of the other victims must have died after a short interval, during which they would have been unconscious.

A 410–TON TRAIN

SUPERINTENDENT AND THE DERAILMENT.

Mr. Robert White Higgins, Exeter, divisional superintendent of the G.W.R., said the 9.50 p.m. train from Paddington reached Taunton at 3.30 a.m. on November 4th. It was scheduled to arrive at 2.22 a.m. There were 13 coaches with 410 tons behind the engine. At 3.43 it left Taunton down relief platform.

At 3.39 the 12.50 a.m. newspaper train from Paddington was accepted on the down main line. It was travelling at a higher rate of speed, and it was estimated that it overhauled the 9.50 train near the Norton Fitzwarren box, about two miles from Taunton. The Norton Fitzwarren starting signals being 'on', the trap would be open and the passenger train was consequently derailed.

The engine and tender (which weighed 135 tons) and six vehicles left the rails. The coaches were of steel.

In reply to Mr. Baty, Mr. Higgins said the train was late because of general conditions – it was a heavy train with a great deal of work to do; there were many stops, and the weather was bad.

APPARATUS IN ORDER.

Mr. Arthur William Burt, 60, Hamilton-road, Taunton, G.W.R. signal and telegraph inspector for the Taunton district, explained the model of the track and signals from Taunton to the scene of the crash. He explained that the relief line signals were on the left of that track, and the main line signals on the right of the main line.

He added that after the accident the signals and line wires and also the automatic train control ramps were in order. The weather could not have affected the action of the signals or ramp. The driver would have warning when he left Taunton that he was on the relief line. He would have four other signals and the automatic ramp against him. If the automatic control was against a driver a siren would sound in his cab and the vacuum brakes would be applied.

In reply to Mr. Baty, Mr. Burt said it was possible to get the siren sounding from the automatic train control ramp when the distance signal was in the off position; but that was not possible in the reverse direction. The failure of the apparatus would tend to pull up the train.

DETONATORS ON THE LINE.

Re-called, Mr. Burt explained the position of three detonators on the Wellington side of Norton. After the accident he found that two had exploded and one had blown out. They were 192 yards from the trap. The detonators should have given the engine driver warning to apply his brakes immediately. Their primary duty was to warn a stationary train about to move off.

In reply to the Coroner, it was explained that when the detonators went off it would be too late for a driver to stop a train travelling at 35 to 40 miles an hour.

SIGNALMEN'S EVIDENCE

WHY RELIEF LINE WAS USED.

Mr. Henry James Wadham, J.P., a special class signalman, of Netherclay Terrace, Bishop's Hull, said on November 3rd he went on duty at 10 p.m., and had sole charge of the Taunton West box. He received the 9.50 passenger train at 3.30 a.m. in its scheduled position – the relief line platform.

At 3.37 he asked for and obtained "line clear" on the down relief line, and lowered his signals accordingly. He had previously given the "line clear" signal to the newspaper train on the main down line. He sent "train entering section" signal to the Taunton West junction box at 3.43, and the train passed witness's box at 3.44.

At 3.50 he received news of the crash from the Norton Fitzwarren signalman, and sent for help.

"STORMY NIGHT."

In reply to Mr. Collins, Mr. Wadham said it was a "fearful" night – it was very stormy and dark, with a gale blowing, and he had difficulty in seeing his signals.

In reply to other questions, Mr. Wadham said that the 9.50 passenger train arrived nearly always on the relief platform and went out on the down main line. On this occasion, however, the train was "out of course" through the black-out, fog, and abnormal conditions. He could not remember having had occasion on any other Sunday night to send the 9.50 train out on the down relief line. The relief line was used, whenever necessary, to expedite traffic. Mr. Walter William Tucker, signalman at Taunton West junction box, of 23, Salisbury-street, Taunton, said he was offered the 9.50 p.m. train on the down relief line at 3.39 a.m. and immediately after was offered the 12.50 a.m. on the down main.

After obtaining "line clear" from the Silk Mills box for both trains, he put down the necessary signals to receive them. He received "out of section" signals from the Silk Mills box at 3.49 a.m.

The passenger train was just leading when the two engines passed his box.

NEWSPAPER TRAIN OVERTAKING.

Mr. Albert Burch, 6, Florence-Terrace, Bishop's Hull, signalman at the Silk Mills box, said he lowered his signals for both trains at 3.41 a.m. They passed the box at 3.49 a.m. It seemed that the newspaper train was rapidly overtaking the other.

Mr. William John Coles, 4, Rectory-road, Norton Fitzwarren, signalman at the Norton Fitzwarren box, said that at 3.39 a.m. he obtaind the "line clear" from the Victory box, and lowered his signals for the newspaper train to precede the passenger train on the main line. All signals on the relief line were at danger.

He added, "I expected the 9.50 train to pull up on the Taunton side of my box. I was surprised to see it passing me at about 40 miles an hour. A few seconds later I heard a crash. I immediately sent out the signal 'Obstruction – Danger' to the Victory and Silk Mills boxes."

In reply to Mr. Baty, witness said the starting signal on the main line near his box was nearly twice as high as that on the relief line, and more easily seen.

DRIVER'S ACTION.

The signalman at the Victory box, Hill-farrance, Mr. William Langford, 16, Wellington New-road, Taunton, said that when he heard of the accident he placed detonators on the up line. During his absence Driver Stacey, of the 9.50 train, came from the scene of the accident, three-quarters of a mile away. He had no light, and it was a mystery how he got there. He left a note saying that he had come to see that the up line was protected, and that he had taken a lamp from the box. Witness returned to his box as Driver Stacey was leaving. His note gave the time as 4.10 a.m.

VIEW RESTRICTED.

Mr. Alexander Christison, divisional locomotive superintendent, described the position of an engine driver and fireman in their cabin. He said the driver remained on the right side of the footplate, and it was part of the fireman's duty to help him to read the signals.

In reply to Mr. Baty, witness said the anti-glare sheets on the engine restricted the driver's view from the side of the cabin. Through the glass screen at the front he would have good visibility to the right, but not to the left.

He added that Driver Stacey had driven over that section for a number of years.

900 PASSENGERS.

Mr. James Winyard, guard on the passenger train, said his van was the eighth coach from the engine. When the train left Taunton he saw no signals, and did not notice whether they were on the main or relief line. The train approached Norton at about 35 miles an hour. It had about 900 passengers.

He added, "There was no panic after the crash, and everyone behaved with complete composure. Help was given by passengers, including members of the Forces, and afterwards by the police, ambulance men, railwaymen, and others. I did not think there was anyone alive in the wreckage half an hour after the crash."

Mr. John Pearce, of Plymouth, the travelling ticket collector on the train, said at Taunton he reminded the driver to stop at Teignmouth. As the train left he saw one green light from the signal. At the time of the crash he was in the coach next to the engine, but escaped with bruises and shock.

ENGINE DRIVER EXPLAINS

THOUGHT A GREEN LIGHT WAS HIS.

The engine driver, Mr. Percy William Stacey, who was formally cautioned, elected to give evidence. He said that before leaving Taunton he saw that the signal from the relief line to the main line was off. After a conversation with the ticket collector, he saw the signal was still off.

"As we moved off," he continued, "I saw a green light, which I thought was mine; I am not sure of that now. I heard the siren at the automatic train control ramp just after leaving Taunton platform. I proceeded on what I thought was the main line to Norton Fitzwarren. On putting my head outside the anti-glare sheet at Norton Station to see the signals for Victory crossing, I saw another train passing on my right-hand side. I immediately shut off steam, applied my brakes, and came off the road at the catch point."

After the accident he went ahead to Victory signal box.

SIGNALS HE OBSERVED.

In reply to the Coroner, Driver Stacey said that from Taunton to Norton all the signals he was observing were on his right-hand side. He was quite emphatic that after hearing the siren he did not again touch the apparatus.

Stacey added that this was the third time he had driven this train on a Sunday, and on the previous occasions he had been on the main line.

The Coroner: Did you receive any communication about signals from your fireman after you left Taunton Station? – No.

Did he look outside the screen during that time? – I cannot remember, but he was certainly looking through his window part of the time.

In reply to the jury, Stacey said the siren indicated that a signal ahead was against him, but as he proceeded he assumed that the track had cleared. He did not receive any warning near the scene of the accident from the automatic train control.

ANGLE OF SIGNALS.

The Coroner: Did it not occur to you that the angle of the signals was rather wider than usual?

Stacey: I am afraid it did not. There was wind and mist and our windows were practically useless. I was getting up speed and seeing the signals, but I cannot say I noticed the slight difference of angle.

In reply to Mr. Baty, the driver said, "After the crash I got out from the top

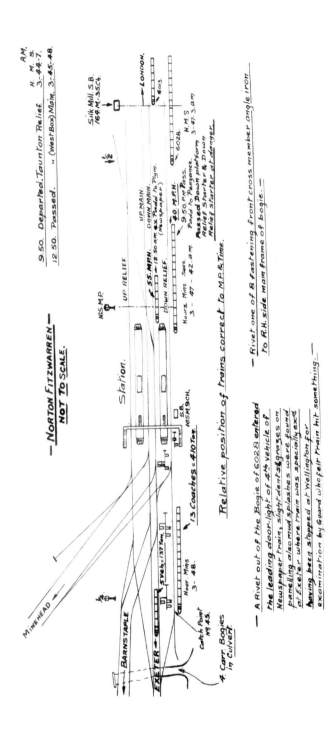

Train movement details prior to the crash.

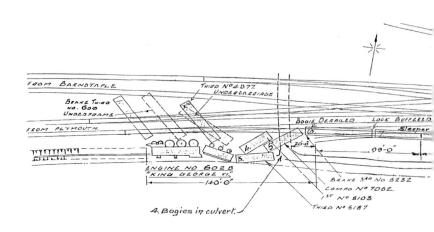

_NORTON
_DERAILMENT OF 9-
_TRAIN ON NOV.
_Scal

Z WARREN.

DDINGTON PASSENGER

O AT 3-48 a.m.

FT = 1 IN

PINEHEAD

TO LONDON

| 00 | 52'0" | Compo 7035 | Third 4326 | Brake Third 1653 | Third 2541. | Third 3920. |
| | | 9 | 10 | 11 | 12 | 13 |

747'-0" From Signal Box.

of the tender, which was then on its side. That put me into a stream up to my waist. I got to the front of the engine and saw what had happened. I immediately went to Victory signal box to see that the up line was protected."

He said he tried to do all that was humanly possible after the crash to protect the line and help in the rescue work.

In reply to a juryman, it was stated that it was left to the discretion of the signalman whether the passenger train should be on the relief line or main line. Ninety-five times out of a hundred it was on the main line and there was no way to communicate this to the driver except by the signals.

CORONER'S COMMENT

HAD THE DRIVER BEEN TOLD.

The Coroner commented, "If only someone had said to the driver at Taunton, 'You are on the relief line to-night,' this accident might never have happened."

The Coroner then addressed the jury, who, after a short retirement, returned the verdict and rider set out above.

The Coroner commended all who took part in the rescue work in conditions which could not well have been worse.

Police-Supt. Edwards also paid tribute to the civilians, railway workers, and others at the scene of the accident, and mentioned especially Driver Stacey, who returned to the wrecked train and rendered valuable service.

Extracted (as written) from the *Somerset County Herald*
Saturday, November 23, 1940

Opposite: One of the first commercial photographs to be taken at first light whilst casualties were still being searched for and before recovery had commenced.

Warrilow, Weston-Super-Mare

Overleaf: A similar view to that on the front cover, but nearer and showing the leading coach bogies being lifted by the recovery crane.

Western Morning News

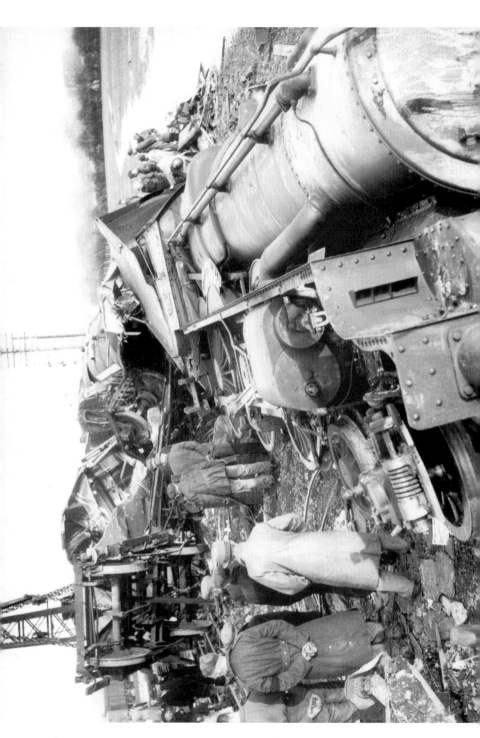

No. 6028 *King George VI*. The fireman was pinned to the side of the cab by spilt coal from the tender and this, together with escaping steam, was the cause of his death.

The locomotive and the end of the second coach. Also shown is the flooded field through which the driver waded in the dark to reach Victory signal box in order to protect the line.

1st Coach. 2nd Coach. 3rd Coach.   4th Coach. Roof
                                    End just visible.

A view looking towards Plymouth from the flooded field showing, as indicated, the first five coaches.

2nd Coach.   5th Coach.   6th Coach.   3rd Coach.

An official photograph similar to that on page 23, but identifying the coaches as they came to rest. The Pioneer Corps helped in the rescue work and clearance of the wreckage.

The leading end of the first coach with the underframe and bogie of the second coach. The underframe of the third coach was approximately 10 feet 6 inches over the top of the tender and about 20 feet from the bed of the stream. Most casualties were in the third coach. Engineman James of Old Oak Common was killed in it. He was relieved at Taunton and was travelling to Exeter to book on to work the return goods to Paddington.

Mr F. Holland, Divisional Engineer, GWR and Mr T. R. Hall, Asst. Divisional Superintendent, Chief Mechanical Engineer's Dept., GWR view the underframe of the first coach laying under the second coach, which has slewed across the tracks.

The 35-ton crane from Newton Abbot prepares another lift among the second, third, fourth and fifth coach wreckage.

Foreman Sendell from the GWR locomotive factory at Newton Abbot supervising the lifting of the frame of the second coach.

The London end of the third coach. No. 5187.

29

A view looking towards Plymouth showing the second and fourth coaches. In the foreground is the track of the Barnstaple branch.

The fourth coach where Engineman James was found in the wreckage.

The lifting of the fourth coach

The London ends of the fourth and fifth coaches strewn across the 'up' and 'down' main lines.

4th Coach.

5th Coach

PADDING

The Swindon crane lifts the fifth coach whilst the Newton Abbot crane tackles what remains of the fourth coach.

The third coach (No. 5187) and the fifth coach (No. 7052) telescoped into one another.

Opposite: Clearance is almost complete. The 'up' road was cleared at 6.30 p.m. on 4th November 1940 and the 'down' road was cleared on the following day at 6.20 p.m. However, debris from the crash still litters the trackside near to where the Minehead branch departed the main line from Taunton.

STOCK DAMAGE REPORT

1st Coach — Brake third No. 609: Body completely off frame. Luggage body end damaged and bulged outwards; both bogies displaced from frame and damaged. Coach lying across 'up' and 'down' main lines.

2nd Coach — Third No. 4377: Body completely off frame and leading end of same damaged at the first compartment. Both bogies displaced from frame and damaged. Coach lying across 'up' and 'down' main lines.

3rd Coach — Third No. 5187: Telescoped both ends, the leading end being over the top of end of engine's tender. Body extensively damaged. Both bogies displaced from frame and extensively damaged.

4th Coach — First No. 8103: Telescoped both ends; body completely off frame; extensively damaged. Both bogies damaged.

5th Coach — Compo. No. 7052: Telescoped leading end; body extensively damaged. Both bogies displaced and damaged.

6th Coach — Third No. 5232: Derailed one bogie. Damaged end; bent headstock. Buffers and dynamo damaged.

7th Coach — First sleeping car No. 9087: Buffers bent; cells broken; main vacuum pipe bent. Stopped.

8th Coach — Brake third No. 5109: Buffers bent; cells broken. First aid cabinet missing. Bent screw connection shackle.

9th Coach — Compo. No. 7035: Lavatory washbasin broken; six cells broken; dynamo belt missing.

10th Coach — Third No. 4326: Broken doorlight; four cells broken; dynamo belt missing.

11th Coach — Brake third No. 1653: Seven cells broken; dynamo belt missing; first aid cabinet missing.

12th Coach — Third No. 2541: Five cells broken.

13th Coach	– Third No. 3920: Arm-rest broken.
Engine	– No. 6028 *King George VI:* Bogie, centre-pin and bracket distorted; bogie carriage requires reconstructing; all brake gear requires overhauling; boiler nil. Cab requires rebuilding; footplate distorted. ATC casting broken. Chimney casting and safety-valve casting damaged. Other minor repairs required. Wheels and frame good and correct to gauge.
Tender	– Brake gear needs overhauling. L.T. axle box and front horn block of same broken. Hole in wall of tank left top corner, and left-hand toolbox damaged; other minor repairs required.

Key to coach construction:–

Third	– All compartments third class passengers.
First	– All compartments first class passengers.
Compo.	– One end first class, remainder third class.
Brake third	– All third class but, in addition, contains a guard's compartment with train-braking equipment, complete with vacuum gauge.
Sleeping car	– First class: contains ten single-berth compartments plus lavatory and attendant's berth. (These coaches were fitted with two six-wheeled bogies as opposed to the usual two four-wheeled bogies of normal passenger coaches.)

Overleaf: The sad and forlorn study of No. 6028 *King George VI* at Taunton Motive Power Depot awaiting transfer to Swindon works for extensive repairs. With the locomotive in this condition, the 'Not to be Moved' sign seemed superfluous!

R.A.E.F. Photographic Artists Taunton
(Courtesy of Richard Mulligan)